USBORNE BIBLE TALES

The Prodigal Son

Retold by Heather Amery
Illustrated by Norman Young

Language consultant: Betty Root
Series editor: Jenny Tyler

This is Jesus.

He told people about God. Some grumbled that he talked to bad people. Jesus told them this story.

There was a rich farmer.

He had two sons who worked with him on his farm.
But one son did not like working.

"I want some money."

"Half of your money will be mine one day," the son said to his father. "I want it now."

The father gave his son the money.

The son took it and soon rode away on his donkey.
His father watched him go. He was very sad.

The son went to the city.

He bought new clothes and a big house. He made lots of new friends and gave parties for them.

The son spent all his money.

He had wasted it all. His friends left him. His clothes and house were sold. He had nothing left.

He was very hungry.

The son begged in the streets for food. Then he got a job looking after some pigs. He was still hungry.

He thought about his father.

"My father's servants always have plenty to eat," he thought. "I'll go home." And off he went.

It was a long journey.

He had to walk all the way. At last, he reached his home. He was tired, dirty and dressed in rags.

The father saw his son.

He ran out to meet him, delighted to see his son again. He hugged and kissed him.

"Forgive me, father."

"It isn't fair for me to be your son anymore," said the son. "Please let me be one of your servants."

The father took him into the house.

He gave his son new clothes and shoes. And he told his servants to make a great feast.

The other son heard the news.

He was very angry. "Father," he said. "I've always worked hard but you never give me anything."

"My dear son," said the father.

"Everything I have is yours. I thought your brother was dead. I'm so happy he's alive and home again."

"God is like that," said Jesus.

"If one bad person changes and becomes good, God forgives him and there is joy in Heaven."